Contents

Living processes

Get started

Can you remember the five life processes for living things?
Use this to help you.

a giraffes   G _ _ _ _ _ _

b ride   R _ _ _ _ _ _ _ _ _ _

c my   M _ _ _ _ _ _

d new   N _ _ _ _ _ _

e skateboard   S _ _ _ _ _ _ _ _ _

---

1 Look at the pictures below – identify the life process that is being shown in each one.

 **a**

 **b**

 **c**

 **d**

 **e**

---

2 Which one of these sentences shows that an oak tree reproduces? Tick one box.

a Leaves fall in autumn. ☐

b Acorns fall off the trees in autumn. ☐

c Leaf buds open in spring. ☐

d Flowers open in spring. ☐

e Leaves produce food through photosynthesis. ☐

On your toes

How does a plant get its nutrients?

_____

_____

Human life cycle

Get started

When human beings are adults they can have babies to make new human beings. Which life process is this?

_____

1 Make a list of three things to show how you have changed since you were a baby.

1 _____

2 _____

3 _____

2 Put these pictures in the right order to show the human life cycle. Number them 1–6.

teenager   adult   foetus   child   baby

  ☐   ☐   ☐   ☐   ☐

3 True or false?

                  True   False

a Humans need help from their parents for many years.   ☐ ☐

b Humans are mammals.   ☐ ☐

c Plants, animals and humans produce young to become adults.   ☐ ☐

d New humans can be created whenadults reach old age.   ☐ ☐

On your toes

What would happen if humans didn't reproduce?

_____

_____

_____

_____

3

Teeth

Get started

We have incisors, canine and molar teeth.
Which teeth have these special jobs?

a cutting _____

b grinding and crushing _____

c ripping and tearing _____

At the dentist's

1 James has gone to the dentist. This is what the dentist can see in James's mouth.

a Colour the incisors red.

b Colour the canines green.

c Colour the molars blue.

2 James asked his friends about how often they clean their teeth. He made a chart of the results of his survey.

a Look at the chart and explain why you think James needed two fillings.

_____

_____

b Which of James's friends is likely to have the healthiest teeth? _____

c Why?_____

_____

name	before breakfast	after breakfast	before tea	before bed
James	✔			
Rita		✔		✔
Debbie	✔		✔	
Scott		✔	✔	
Sally				✔

On your toes

Make a list of three foods that will help James to keep his teeth healthy.

1 _____

2 _____

3 _____

DON'T FORGET

When sugary food is left on and around our teeth, bacteria feed on it and form plaque. This rots away the enamel on our teeth.

Food

Get started

We should have an adequate and varied diet.
What does a 'varied diet' mean?

1 Complete this table.

Food group	Reason why we need them	Found in
Proteins		
Carbohydrates		pasta, bread, potatoes, rice
Fats and oils	to give energy and to keep our bodies working well	
Vitamins and minerals		
Fibre		fruit and vegetables, bread, some breakfast cereals

2 Missing food groups.

a Walter eats chocolate, fried eggs, sausages and ice cream.
Which food groups are missing from his diet?

_____

and _____

b Amy eats apples, orange juice, bran flakes and pasta.
Which food groups are missing from her diet?

_____

and _____

On your toes

What happens if you eat more food than you use for exercising and activity?

_____

_____

Body organs

Get started

Sort these letters to make a word to finish the sentence. **n u c t i n f o**

An organ is a part of the body which has a special _ _ _ _ _ _ _ _ _.

This means it has a special job to do.

1 Which is which?

DON'T FORGET

The digestive system includes a number of separate organs, such as the stomach, small intestine and large intestine.

The main organs of the human body are:

> brain   kidney   lung
> digestive system   heart   liver

Look at the picture opposite. Write the correct position in the table next to each organ.

organ	position	function
Lungs		
Heart		
Brain	1	
Liver		
Kidney		a
Digestive system		

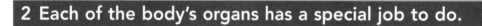

2 Each of the body's organs has a special job to do.

Choose the correct letter for each organ in the table. Write the letters in the function column of the table.

a This cleans the blood and makes waste substances.

b This controls the whole body by sending messages.

c This pumps blood around the body.

d This stores and controls chemicals.

e This takes in oxygen from the air into the blood and gets rid of carbon dioxide, which the body doesn't need.

f This breaks down food so the goodness from it can be carried in the bloodstream to the rest of the body.

On your toes

Look at the table. Which two organs come in pairs?

1 _____

2 _____

The heart

Get started

This diagram represents how blood is circulated around the body.

Draw in arrows to show how the blood is pumped around the body. The first one has been done for you.

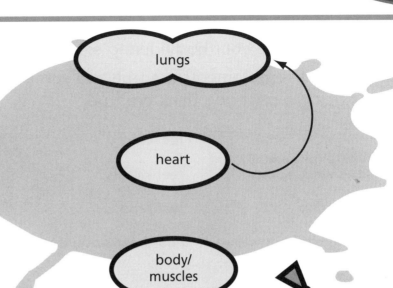

1 Circulation of blood

These phrases have been put in the wrong order. Put a number in the box to show the correct order.

a The blood, containing the oxygen, goes back to the heart.

b The heart pumps the blood to the lungs. `1`

c The muscles and organs use up the oxygen.

d The blood picks up oxygen in the lungs.

e Blood which is now low in oxygen returns to the heart in veins.

f The heart pumps the blood back to the lungs to pick up more oxygen.

g The heart pumps the blood containing oxygen through arteries around the body to the muscles and organs.

On your toes

Name two things the blood takes around the body.

1

2 _____

DON'T FORGET

The blood has to be pumped from the lungs back to the heart before it is pumped around the rest of the body.

Pulse rate

Get started

What happens to your body during exercise?

Some of these statements are true and some are false. Tick the ones you think are true.

muscles work harder		feel cold		
muscles work slower		feel sweaty		
muscles relax		feel tired		body uses up oxygen to give energy
breathing slows down		heartbeat slows down		blood is pumped faster
breathing gets faster		heartbeat gets faster		blood is pumped slower
feel hot		body makes oxygen		

1 Investigating pulse rate

Class 6 have been investigating the effect of exercise on the pulse rate.

Here is a graph showing their results:

They decided to measure their pulse rate after they had been sitting reading, walking or skipping for two minutes.

They measured their pulse rate as soon as they finished their activity, then every minute for four minutes.

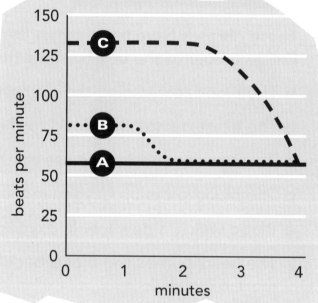

a Write on the graph to show what each line represents – sitting, reading, skipping or walking.

b Explain how you decided which line resulted from each activity.

_____

_____

_____

_____

On your toes

Why do we breathe faster when we exercise?

_____

_____

_____

_____

The skeleton

Get started

Which part of the skeleton protects each of these organs? Draw an arrow to match them to their partner.

brain	ribs
spinal cord	skull
heart	backbone

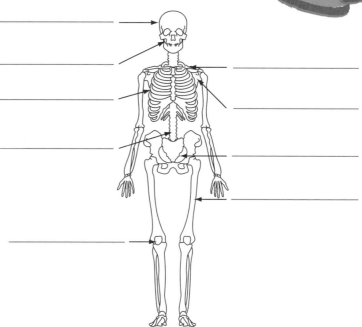

1 'Them bones'

Use the words below to label parts of this skeleton.

skull   back bone   ribs   jaw   shoulder blade   collar bone
pelvis   thigh bone   kneecap

Inside or outside?

One of the other main jobs of the skeleton is to help the body keep its shape.

Some animals have their skeletons on the inside of their body. These are called **endoskeletons**.

Some animals have their skeletons on the outside of their body. These are called **exoskeletons**.

2 Look at the animals below and sort them into two groups.

Colour those with endoskeletons blue and those with exoskeletons red.

On your toes

What are the three functions of the skeleton?

1 To protect vital organs.
2 To support the body.

3 _____

_____

9

Moving muscles

Get started

Fill the spaces in these sentences. Use these words.

> muscles   faster   pull   rate   blood   food

a Bones cannot move on their own, so _____ are attached to them.

b When your muscles _____ on bones, you are able to move.

c When we exercise, our muscles need more _____ flowing to them to bring oxygen and _____ to make energy.

d This means your heart has to beat _____ and therefore your pulse _____ increases.

---

1 Muscles always work in pairs. When one muscle contracts, the other relaxes.

Choose the correct word to finish each sentence.

a The muscle which is paired with the triceps to bend and straighten the arm is the: biceps/bicycle/binocular.

b When a muscle contracts it becomes: longer/thicker/softer.

c When a muscle relaxes it becomes: harder/softer/thicker.

d When you exercise, your muscles need more: carbon dioxide/oxygen/nitrogen.

To help you

Put your hand underneath a table and push up. Feel your arm to see which muscle is contracting. Then put the back of your hand on top of the table and push down. Which muscle is contracting now?

---

2 Colour the muscles that are relaxed in blue and the muscles that are contracted in red.

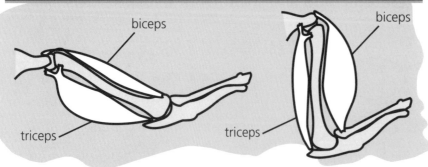

biceps

triceps

biceps

triceps

On your toes

When you exercise what do your muscles need to help them work harder? _____

Dangerous drugs

Get started

True or false?

	True	False
a Alcohol and cigarettes are not types of drugs.		
b All drugs are dangerous if they are not used properly.		
c You cannot become addicted to smoking tobacco.		

1 Warning posters.

Imran saw these posters in the doctors' surgery:

SMOKING KILLS

DON'T PLAY WITH DRUGS

DON'T DRINK AND DRIVE

Choose the correct information for each poster.

a This can damage the liver and it slows down reaction times.

b This can increase the risk of lung cancer. It may also cause heart disease.

c These are helpful when given by a doctor, but it's dangerous to misuse them.

DON'T FORGET

Having a balanced, varied diet and exercising regularly also keeps you healthy.

On your toes

Cigarettes are made from dried, shredded leaves. What are these leaves called?

_____

Leaves

Get started

Choose the best words to finish each sentence:

a The source of energy that leaves can trap is the: rain/sun/wind.

b Leaves are very important to the plant because they:
make food/keep the plant dry/attract bees.

c The green substance inside the leaf is: chlorine/chocolate/chlorophyll.

d If you put a plant into a dark area, the leaves will turn:
brown/yellow/green.

1 Class 5 investigated what plants need to grow well.

The class grew some plants for four weeks. The plants were
put into these four different positions to see what would happen:

| **1** on the window sill of the classroom, with water | **2** on the window sill of the classroom, without water | **3** in the fridge | **4** in the big cupboard in the classroom |

a Which plant do you think will grow best? _____

b Why do you think this one will grow the best?

_____

c What do you think will happen to the leaves on the plant in position **2**?

_____

d What do you think will happen to the leaves on the plant in position **4**?

_____

e Make a list of the conditions that plants need to grow well.

_____

On your toes

Class 5 went to a greenhouse to choose plants for their test.
List two things they should think about so that their test will be fair.

_____

Roots and stem

Get started

Different parts of a plant have special jobs to do.
Which part of a plant does each of these jobs?

a Makes food for new growth using energy from the sun. _____

b Anchors the plant in the soil. _____

c Attracts insects so that pollination can take place. _____

d Supports the flower and transports water
and minerals to other parts of the plant. _____

e Where the seeds are formed. _____

1 Coloured celery

Daniel wanted to find out what would happen if he put a stick of celery in some coloured water. He split the celery and put one side in blue ink and one side in red ink. He left the celery overnight to see what happened.

a What do you think happened to the celery?

_____

b Why do you think this happened?

_____

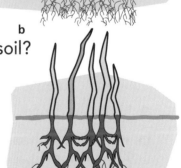

blue ink   red ink

2 Roots

One of these grasses grows in dry, sandy conditions.

a Which one do you think it is, a or b?

b Why do you think that this grass grows in dry, sandy soil?

_____

c What two functions do the roots have?

_____

_____

a

b

On your toes

What is the main root of a carrot called?

_____

13

Revise wise

Get started

Why do many flowers have bright coloured petals?

_____

1 True or false?

	True	False
a Flowers have bright coloured petals so that humans will pick them.		
b The sepals were closed to make a case around the flower when it was a bud.		
c Trees never have flowers.		

2 Anne has taken a tulip flower to pieces and stuck the different parts on a piece of card.

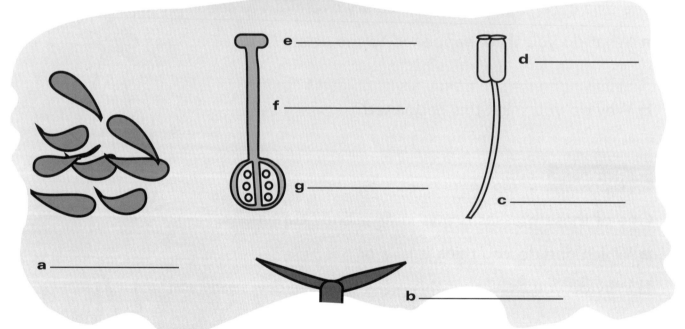

e _____

f _____

d _____

g _____

c _____

a _____

b _____

a Help Anne to label each part of the flower with its proper name.

b The flower has male and female parts. Put a letter **M** beside the male parts and a letter **F** beside the female parts.

On your toes

Which part of the flower turns into the seeds?

_____

_____

Pollination

Get started

a Which part of the plant carries the pollen? _____

b Does the pollen come from a male or female part of the flower? _____

c Which part of the plant does the pollen 'stick' to? _____

d What does the pollen help create? _____

1 Put these pictures in order.

Write the numbers in the boxes.
The first one is done for you.

			1

What is happening in each picture?

picture a _____

picture b _____

picture c _____

picture d _____

2 What is Tom doing?

Tom can be seen in his greenhouse in the summer with a very fine paintbrush. He brushes the inside of one tomato flower and then another tomato flower. What is he doing?

_____

_____

Name two ways this process can happen in the wild.

_____

_____

On your toes

What is created when pollen joins together with ovules?

_____

_____

_____

Fertilisation

Get started

True or false?

	True	False
a Insects help some plants to reproduce.		
b Fertilisation occurs when pollen is transferred from one flower to another.		
c The ovary gets bigger and bigger to become a fruit.		

1 Life cycle of a plant

Class 6 planted some seeds.
Oliver drew pictures of his plant to record its growth.

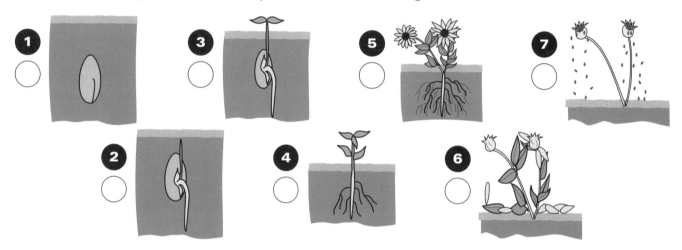

Here are Oliver's notes. Which picture does each sentence describe?

Write the letters in the circles by the pictures.

a The fruit is ripe and has exploded. Individual seeds are dispersed.

b The petals on the flowers attract insects which take the pollen from one flower to another.

c The seed needs water and warmth to grow.

d The seed produces a root and a shoot.

e After fertilisation the petals fall and the ovary swells to form a fruit.

f As the plant grows taller it produces more leaves and the root system starts to spread out.

g The shoot grows enough to push up above the soil.

On your toes

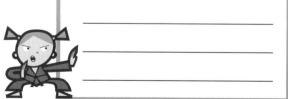

What do the ovules become after they have been fertilised?

_____

_____

_____

Seed dispersal

Get started

Look at this list.

Underline the seeds in blue. Underline the fruits in red.

Be careful! Some of these are not fruits or seeds.

celery   lettuce   pea   lemon   potato   peanut

apple   radish   carrot   tomato   cucumber

cabbage   beetroot   cauliflower   rhubarb   bean

1 Here are three of the different ways that seeds are dispersed:

1 by animals
2 by wind
3 by exploding mechanisms in the fruit.

How are these seeds dispersed? Write the correct number in the circles by the pictures. Under each picture explain how the structure of the fruit enables this to happen.

DON'T FORGET

Seeds need to move away from the parent plant so that they have enough light, warmth and water.

a ○

_____

_____

b ○
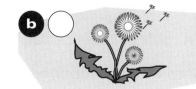

_____

_____

c ○

_____

_____

d ○
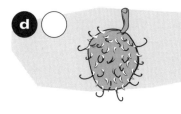

_____

_____

e ○

_____

_____

f ○

_____

_____

On your toes

How are the seeds from grass dispersed?

_____

Growing seeds

Revise wise

Get started

Which of these things do seeds need in order to start to germinate?

water ☐   soil ☐   air ☐   warmth ☐   light ☐

1 The competition

David and Ellie are both given some cress seeds.

David places his seeds in a pot of damp soil.
He covers the pot with a polythene bag and leaves it on a window sill.

Ellie also places her seeds in a pot of damp soil, but she covers her pot with some black plastic from a bin liner.

DON'T FORGET

Seeds do not need light in order to start to grow.

After a few days, the children look at their seedlings.

a Whose seedlings are likely to have the longest stems? _____

b Whose seedlings are likely to have the greenest leaves? _____

c The person whose seedlings have the longest stems is very pleased. The longest seedlings must be the healthiest! Is this person right? Explain your answer.

_____

_____

_____

_____

On your toes

What is the name of the substance that gives leaves their green colour?_____

Sorting animals 1

Get started

An animal with a back bone is a **vertebrate**.

An animal without a backbone is called _____ .

1 What's wrong?

Re-write these statements so that they are true.

a Reptiles lay their eggs in water.

_____

_____

b Young amphibians breathe through lungs.

_____

_____

c Fish have a body covering of hair or fur.

_____

_____

d Mammals lay eggs on land.

_____

_____

e Birds are unable to control the temperature of the inside of their bodies. They are cold blooded.

_____

_____

_____

_____

On your toes

What is special about the way in which mammals feed their young?

_____

Sorting animals 2

Get started

Sort these letters to make a word to finish the sentence.

ICY FIN GLASS

Sorting living things by looking at how they are similar or different is called C _ _ _ _ _ _ _ _ _ _ _ _ _ .

1 What on earth is it?

Professor Donothing has recently been on safari to a strange and distant island. Here are pictures of five of the animals he found.

a   b   c   d   e

Use this key to identify them.

Does the animal have wings?

yes — no

Does it have a long neck?   Does it have a pouch for young?

yes — no   yes — no

running beaker   furry whistler   woolly leaper   Does it have a beak?

yes — no

sleepy bird brain   big snapper

Write the name of each animal here:

a _____

b _____

c _____

d _____

e _____

On your toes

Following a key is easy. The answer to every question is either _____ or _____ .

Get started

a The kind of surroundings that plants and animals live in are called

e _ _ _ _ _ _ _ _ _ t s .

b The exact place where a plant or animal lives is its h _ _ _ _ _ t .

c The way in which a plant or animal is specially designed for its way of life

is called a _ _ _ _ _ _ _ _ _ n .

---

1 These animals are in the wrong habitats.

Give two reasons why each animal would not survive in the habitat shown.

a _____

_____

_____

_____

b _____

_____

_____

_____

---

2 Very few predators successfully attack hedgehogs.

Describe two ways in which
the hedgehog defends itself.

_____

_____

_____

_____

3 How are seals designed for swimming in cold seas?

Describe two ways.

_____

_____

_____

_____

On your toes

True or false?

                                                 True   False

a The front legs of bats are adapted for flying.

b The front legs of kangaroos are adapted for jumping.

Food chains

Get started

Arrange these animals and plants into a simple food chain.

insect
sparrow hawk
leaves
shrew

▲

▲

▲

DON'T FORGET

In a food chain the arrows point to the eaters.

1 Tick the right word to describe each animal or plant.

a lettuce   [ ] carnivore   [ ] herbivore   [ ] producer

b rabbit   [ ] carnivore   [ ] herbivore   [ ] producer

c tiger   [ ] predator   [ ] prey   [ ] producer

2 Producer or consumer?

Write a P next to the producer, and a C next to the consumer in each of these pairs.

a [ ] wheat grains   [ ] chicken

b [ ] hamster   [ ] sunflower seeds

c [ ] termite   [ ] piece of wood

d [ ] bamboo shoots   [ ] giant panda

3 A scientist counted the numbers of barn owls and the numbers of fieldmice on a farm.

Which number was the greatest – barn owls or fieldmice? _____

Why do you think this?

_____

_____

On your toes

Why are plants called the producers in food chains?

_____

Get started

Add the missing words to complete each sentence.

a Oil spills are a kind of p _ _ _ _ _ _ _ _ _ .

b The Bengal tiger is an endangered

s _ _ _ _ _ _ .

c Mountain gorillas could soon become

e _ _ _ _ _ _ .

DON'T FORGET

Just one change in a habitat can affect all the plants and animals in it.

1 What is wrong in each of these pictures?

a   **b**   **c**   rare orchids

_____   _____   _____

_____   _____   _____

_____   _____   _____

2 What is happening?

a What are these people doing?

Empty Bottles

_____

_____

b Why is it a good idea?

_____

_____

_____

On your toes

Why are paper bags more 'environmentally friendly' than plastic ones?

_____

Micro-organisms

Get started

True or false?

	True	False
a All micro-organisms are very dangerous.		
b Some micro-organisms are used in making foods.		
c Micro-organisms do not like to be kept warm.		

1 Micro-problem

Yeast is a living organism. It grows, reproduces and needs food.

Yeast is used to make bread rise. It breaks down sugar and releases carbon dioxide.

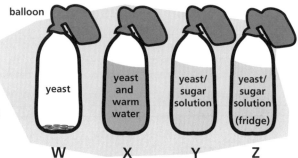

balloon

yeast | yeast and warm water | yeast/sugar solution | yeast/sugar solution (fridge)

W   X   Y   Z

James and Selena put some yeast, water and sugar in small plastic bottles as shown in the picture.
They put flask Z in the fridge and all the rest in a warm place.
After just a short while they looked at flask Y and saw bubbles in the liquid.

a What gas do you think the bubbles were? _____

After an hour, the children looked at all the flasks again.

b What do you think was happening in flask W, and why?

_____

c What do you think was happening in flask X, and why?

_____

d What do you think the children saw when they compared flasks Y and Z?

_____

_____

The children could have set up another flask to see if yeast can break down sugar without water.

e What would they have put in it?

_____

_____

On your toes

Why should you always wash your hands before cooking?

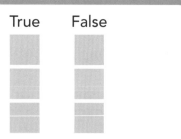

_____

_____

What is it made from?

Get started

Objects are _____ _____ materials.

1 Join each material to the correct sorting hoop.

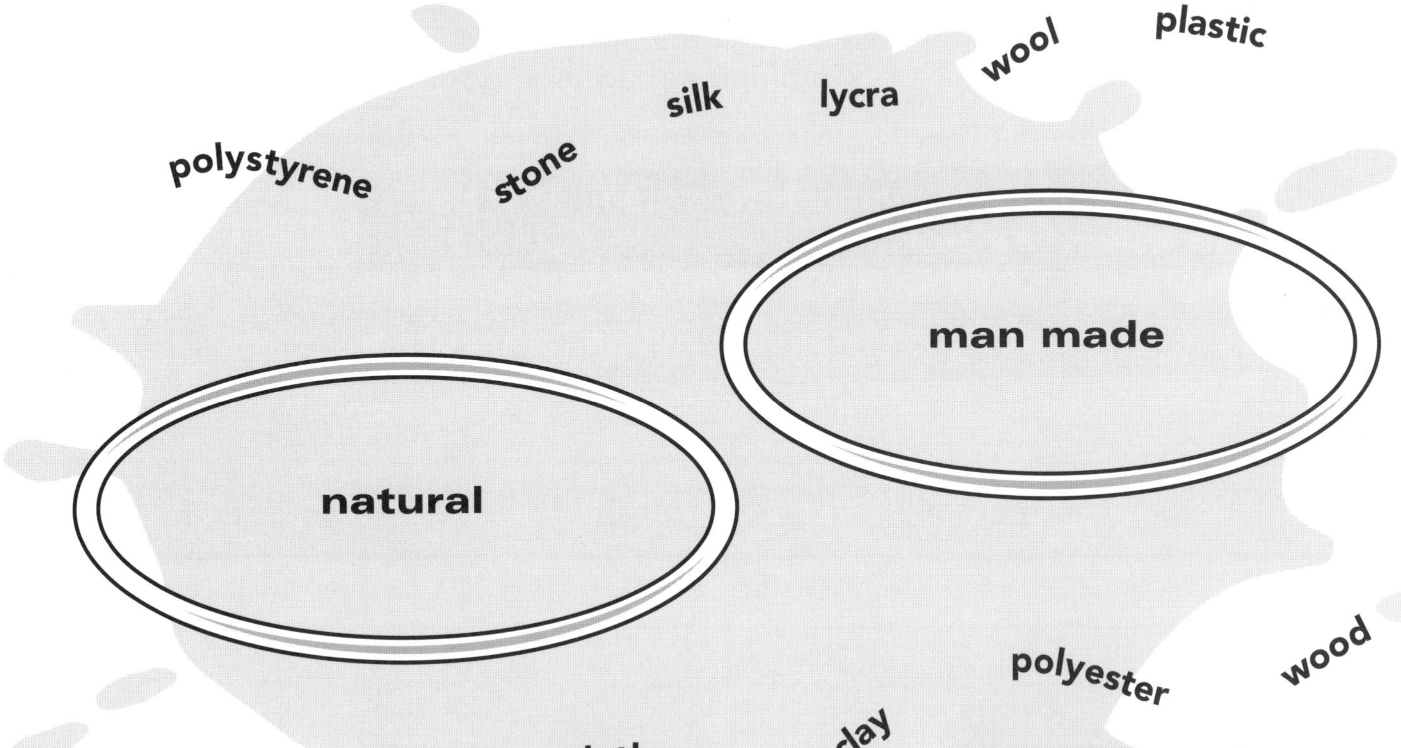

wool

plastic

silk   lycra

polystyrene   stone

man made

natural

polyester   wood

polythene   clay

shell   nylon

2 Processed materials

Some natural materials are processed.

Underline the correct ending for each of these sentences.

a Bricks are made from clay which has been: cooled/soaked/fired.

b Paper is made from wood which has been: burnt and soaked/minced and soaked/ frozen and soaked.

c Glass is made from sand which has been: heated/crushed/compressed.

On your toes

What is a synthetic material?

_____

_____

_____

25

Choosing the right material

Get started

Join each material to a suitable purpose:

a silk   making a mop

b steel   making a tie

c towelling   making a CD case

d plastic   making a magnetic door catch

---

1 Choose one of these materials to write in each box of the materials matrix.

slate   carpet wool   polythene   ribbon   sandpaper   glass

	transparent	rough	smooth
hard			
soft			

---

2 Choose one of the suggested words to describe each of these material sets.

a rubber band, lycra, elastic

These materials are all _____ .
(stretchy/soft/rough)

b glass, polythene, cellophane

These materials are all _____ .
(brittle/heavy/transparent)

c lead, granite, wet clay

These materials are all _____ .
(flexible/heavy/hard)

On your toes

The ways that a material appears and behaves are its

p _ _ _ _ _ _ _ _ _ _ .

Revise wise

Get started

Underline the correct ending for this sentence:

Heat always travels from cold to hot/hot to cold.

1 Hot stuff! True or false?

	True	False
a A material that heat travels through easily is an insulator.		
b Wool is a good insulator.		
c Metals are usually good conductors of heat.		
d It is a good idea to stir a pan of hot water with a metal spoon.		
e If you wrap a hot water bottle with a blanket it will stay hot for longer.		
f Wood is a poor conductor.		
g Metals are usually poor insulators.		

2 Who's right?

If I wrap my lolly in newspaper it will stay frozen for longer.

Don't be silly. It will get warm and melt faster.

Rob   **Andy**

DON'T FORGET

A good conductor is a poor insulator.

I think _____ is right, because:

_____

_____

On your toes

Which material would you use to make a handle for a kettle, plastic or aluminium? _____

Rocks

Get started

Underline the best word to finish this sentence.

Everywhere on Earth, even on the sea bed, there are rocks under the covers/ground/water.

1 Rock and roll!

We use rocks in lots of different ways. Choose a set of words from this list to describe why each rock is chosen for the use shown.

hard-wearing and strong   hard and beautifully coloured
soft and white   smooth and breaks into flat pieces

a Slate is _____ .

b Chalk is _____ .

c Marble is _____ .

d Granite is _____ .

2 Underline the right word to finish each sentence.

a Water will soak through a rock which is permeable/impermeable.

b Water will make puddles on a rock which is permeable/impermeable.

3 Which is the hardest?

Liz and Amy were testing some rocks to see which was the hardest. The rocks were labelled A, B and C. They found that:

- rock A scratched rock C but not rock B
- rock B scratched rock A and rock C.

a Which rock was the hardest? ▢

b Which rock was the softest? ▢

On your toes

What do you call the evidence of animal or plant remains sometimes found in rocks?

_____

_____

_____

Soil

Get started

Complete these sentences. Soil is a mixture of:

a tiny pieces of broken down _____

b remains of dead _____ and _____

c a _ _ _ in spaces

d and w _ _ _ _ _ (makes soil damp).

1 Soil selection

Lady Veryrich's jewels were stolen. After a long search, the police found them hidden in a box in a wood. The soil in the wood was a heavy clay.

Two well-known criminals, Burglar Ben and Burglar Bob, were suspects. The police took samples of soil from their boots.

The soil from Burglar Bob's boots contained gritty particles. Water drained through it easily. The soil from Burglar Ben's boots contained tiny particles. Water did not drain through it well.

Which burglar is more likely to have stolen the jewels?

_____

Burglar **Bob**

Burglar **Ben**

2 Soil and water

Ayesha put some soil and water in a lidded jar and shook it.
She left it for a little while andthen looked at the layers that had settled.

a What part of the soil do you think she might see at the bottom of the jar?

_____

_____

b What part of the soil might be floating on the top of the water?

_____

_____

On your toes

Plants take nutrients (food) from the soil through their roots. Although these nutrients are now in water, which part of the soil did they originally come from?

_____

Get started

1 Try these!

Join each material to the correct label.

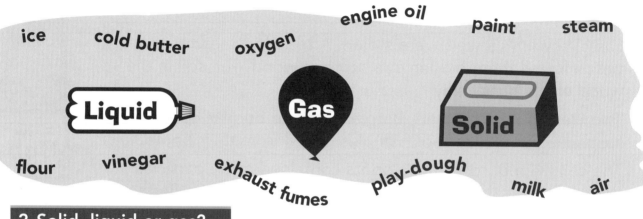

ice   cold butter   oxygen   engine oil   paint   steam

Liquid   **Gas**   **Solid**

flour   vinegar   exhaust fumes   play-dough   milk   air

2 Solid, liquid or gas?

There are three materials on the worktop in a kitchen.

a Material X is in a bowl. Its surface is flat. By tipping the bowl, the material can be moved into another container. Its surface becomes flat again.

This material is a _____ .

b Material Y is also in a bowl. Its surface is flat. If the bowl is tipped right over, the material falls out and now its upper surface is round.

This material is a _____ .

c Material Z is in a special container. If there was to be a fire in the kitchen this material could be used to put the fire out. A trigger on the container allows a cloud of the material to escape.

This material is a _____ .

On your toes

You can pour sand, but is it a solid or a liquid? _____

Reversible changes

Get started

a When a liquid is heated it can turn into a _____ .

b When a liquid is cooled it can turn into a _____ .

1 Un-muddle the letters to make one word to finish each sentence.

a When water turns into steam, this is called _____ .

b When ice turns into liquid water, this is called _____ .

c When steam turns into liquid water, this is called _____ .

d When liquid water turns into ice, this is called _____ .

e Puddles and washing can dry as water particles drift into the air. This is called _____ .

big lion

mint gel

conned sign

green fiz

root a van pie

2 What is happening to water in each of these pictures?

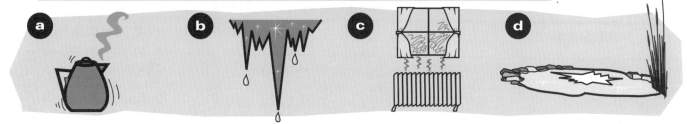

a _____   **b** _____   **c** _____   **d** _____

3 Each of these sentences has an incorrect word. Write the correct word.

a Water from the surface of the sea *freezes* to form clouds.

_____

b Clouds drift over the land and the water *evaporates* to form rain.

_____

c Rain water reaches rivers which carry it back to the *mountains*.

_____

On your toes

Which is hotter, steam or water vapour?

_____

DON'T FORGET

A reversible change is one which can be undone.

Get started

A change which cannot be undone is called irreversible or permanent.

a Some materials burn if they are strongly heated.

This change is _____ . (reversible/permanent)

b Some materials change into a new material when they are heated.

This change is _____ . (reversible/permanent)

1 Look at the changes which have happened to materials in each picture.

Each change has been caused by heating or cooling. Can the change be reversed? Tick the right box under each picture.

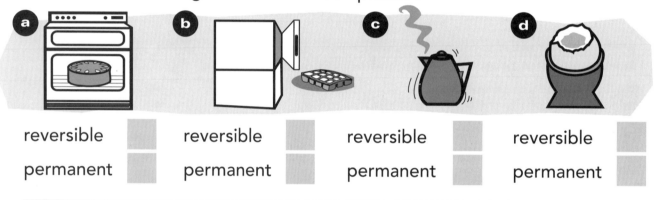

| reversible | reversible | reversible | reversible |
| permanent | permanent | permanent | permanent |

2 How many reversible changes of materials can you spot in this story? Put a ring around each one.

We were lost on the planet Zog. The heating failed in our space craft and it was so cold that the alpha fuel froze in the fuel pods. Then one day a huge new sun rose in the sky. We went outside. It was so hot that the water was boiling in the marshes around us. Steam hit the windows of our craft and condensed into streams of water. Even the metal shields were melting. Liquid metal dripped down onto the broken radio. It must have somehow solidified again across the broken connection, because all of a sudden we heard a voice calling 'Come in Space Craft Zero'.

Rescue was on the way!

On your toes

A permanent change is reversible. True or false? _____

32

Mixing materials

Get started

When you put sugar into warm water it will seem to disappear.

True or false? _____

1 Choose the right word to finish each sentence.

a A teaspoon of salt will seem to disappear when it is stirred in a glass of warm water. This is called dissolving/melting.

b The clear liquid that is made when this happens is called a potion/solution.

c Solids which seem to 'disappear' in liquids are called magic/soluble.

d Sand does not mix with water in this way. It can still be seen and does not change in appearance. Sand is insoluble/heavy.

2 What will happen?

a Here is a glass of warm water. A teaspoonful of an insoluble green powder is added to it. Draw what will happen.

b Here is a glass of warm water. A teaspoonful of a soluble green powder is added to it. Draw what will happen.

DON'T FORGET

When a solid dissolves in a liquid the mixture is called a solution.

On your toes

Solids often dissolve better in warm water than in cold. True or false? _____

33

Separating mixtures

Get started

What are the three main methods that you can use to separate mixtures?

a S _ _ _ _ _ _

b F _ _ _ _ _ _ _ _ _

c E _ _ _ _ _ _ _ _ _ _

DON'T FORGET

A filter is really just a sieve with very tiny holes.

1 True or false?

	True	False
a You can separate soil from pebbles by sieving.		
b You can separate sand from peas by filtering.		
c You can separate salt from sea water by sieving.		
d You can separate tea leaves from water by filtering.		

2 Rock salt challenge

Look at these drawings of an experiment to get salt from rock salt (a mixture of salt, tiny bits of gravel, and sand).

Write what is happening. Be clear at each stage what is being separated from what.

a _____

_____

b _____

_____

c _____

_____

d _____

_____

e _____

_____

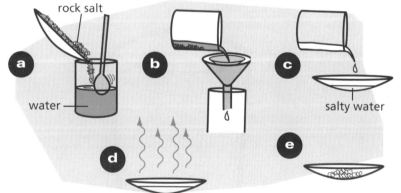

rock salt

water

salty water

a **b** **c** **d** **e**

On your toes

Choose the missing word.

If you keep adding sugar to warm water and stirring it, you will notice that after a while the sugar stops dissolving.

The solution you have made is _____ . (satisfied/saturated)

Get started

In this space, draw a simple series circuit with a cell, a bulb and a switch. Show the switch on and the bulb lit.

1 Circuit puzzles.

a Here's a circuit drawing with something missing. Draw something in the space that would make the bulb **dimmer**.

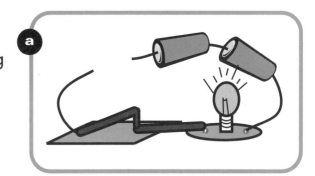

b Here's another circuit drawing with something missing. Draw something in the space that would make the bulb **brighter**.

c To make a bulb brighter in a series circuit, you can add more _____ .

To make the bulb dimmer, you could add a _____ or a _____ .

d In this circuit, show where you would connect a wire to the resistance wire to make the bulb light brightly. Label the wire (a).

Then show where you would connect your wire to the resistance wire if you wanted to make the bulb light dimly. Label this wire (b).

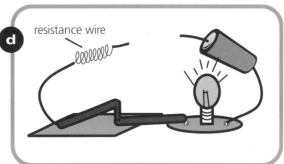

resistance wire

DON'T FORGET

Bulbs usually become dimmer if you add more parts to a circuit.

On your toes

How could you make a switch to use if you wanted to leave a bulb on for a long time?

_____

Circuit diagrams

Get started

Do it with diagrams.

Can you work out why the bulb in this circuit does not light, even though the switch is on?

_____

_____

---

1 Draw lines to match the words to the symbols.

battery   bulb   switch – off   switch – on   buzzer   motor

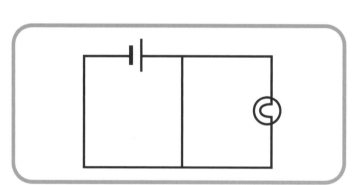

---

2 Alfie made a circuit like this.

His teacher tells him that this is not a safe circuit. What is wrong?

_____

_____

_____

---

3 Describe this circuit. The first bit is done for you.

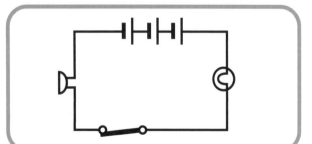

This circuit has three cells

connected to . . .

_____

_____

On your toes

What is a series circuit?

_____

DON'T FORGET

Use straight lines when you draw wires in circuit diagrams.

Get started

Write four things that can happen when forces are at work.

Forces can make things _____ .

Forces can make things _____ .

Forces can make things _____ .

Forces can make things _____ .

> **DON'T FORGET**
>
> A force is just a push or a pull. Gravity is a downwards pull.

What's happening?

a Sometimes nothing is happening, but forces are still acting. Lean on a wall. You don't go move, but your weight is pushing against the wall and the force of reaction from the wall is acting to balance your weight. Draw yourself leaning on the wall. Draw arrows to show the force of your weight and the force of reaction.

b If you can, find an air-filled ball. Drop it from your hand. It falls to the floor, doesn't it? Now drop it (gently!) into a sink or bowl of water. It doesn't fall to the bottom of the sink because of upthrust from the water. Push gently on the ball and you will feel the upthrust.

Draw the ball in the water. Draw arrows to show the equal and opposite forces of gravity and upthrust that are acting on the ball.

c Jen hangs a toy car on an elastic band and measures how much the band stretches.

When she dangles the car in a glass of water, she notices that the band doesn't stretch as much. Why is this?

_____

_____

On your toes

Upthrust can push upwards or downwards. True or false? _____

Opposite forces

Get started

Underline the correct word in the sentence.

When something is slowing down, friction/gravity is the main force that is making it happen.

1 Draw a picture to show each thing that is happening.

Think how you will show the size of the forces that are acting on objects . . .

a

. . . speeding up.

_____

b

. . . completely still on the ground.

_____

c

. . . slowing down.

_____

d

. . . floating in water.

_____

2 On each of these pictures, draw arrows to show the forces that are acting. Remember to use larger arrows for larger forces.

On your toes

True or false: in any situation, there is usually more than one force operating.

38

Gravity

Get started

Use one of these words to fill in each space:

centre   orbit   attraction   pull   orbit

a Gravity is a force of _____ between objects.

b Gravity is the force that keeps the Earth in _____ around the sun, and also keeps the moon in _____ around the Earth.

c On Earth, gravity acts to _____ all objects towards the _____ of the Earth.

1 Matters of gravity. The pull of gravity gives objects their weight.

In the solar system, the bigger the planet, the bigger the pull of gravity, so you would weigh more on big planets than on small planets.

Look at this information about some of the planets in our solar system and work out on which planet you would weigh the most.

The Earth is bigger than Mars. Mercury is smaller than Mars. Venus is bigger than Mars and Mercury, but smaller than the Earth.

I'd weigh the most on _____ because _____

_____

2 Look at this picture. How many examples of gravity in action can you see?

☐ examples

On your toes

Gravity gives you your mass. True or false? _____

39

Friction and air resistance

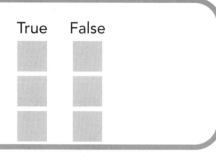

Get started

True or false?

	True	False
a Without friction, it would be easier for shoes to grip the ground.		
b Friction is a force that acts against movement.		
c Friction is another name for the force of gravity.		

1 Oliver's bar graph

Oliver carries out an investigation in which he drags a brick across different surfaces. He measures the force needed to drag the brick using a Newton meter.

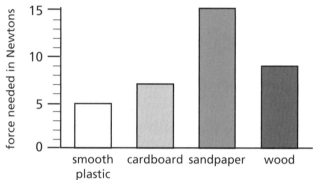

a What does the graph tell you about the force of friction between the different surfaces and the brick?

_____

b Which surface created the most frictional force? _____

2 Parachute investigation

Emily and Noel carry out an investigation on parachutes.

They change the size of their parachute and measure how long it takes for it to fall to the ground. Here are their results:

Size of parachute (cm)	10 × 10	15 × 15	20 × 20	25 × 25
Time taken to fall (s)	6	8.5	11	13.5

a What size was the parachute which fell the most slowly? _____

b Why do you think this parachute was the slowest?

_____

_____

On your toes

How do aircraft reduce air resistance?

_____

Get started

Arrows are used to show both the size and direction of forces.

What do these arrows tell you about the forces acting on this toy?

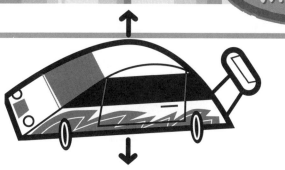

_____

1 More forces

The units used to measure the size of forces are named after a famous scientist. Tick the name of the correct scientist:

☐ Alexander Fleming   ☐ Albert Einstein

☐ Isaac Newton   ☐ Charles Darwin

2 To make them precise, the arrows showing forces can be drawn to scale.

Here are several force arrows. The scale is 1 cm = 1 newton (1N). Measure the arrows and write how big each force is next to them.

a _____   **b** _____   **c** _____   **d** _____

3 Here a football is being kicked.

Draw arrows to show each of these forces.

Label your arrows, a, b, c, d.

a The force that pushes the ball forward.

b The force of gravity.

c The force of reaction from the ground.

d The force of air resistance.

On your toes

What's the odd word out?

☐ force   ☐ newton   ☐ gravity   ☐ circuit   ☐ friction

Magnets

Get started

Put a ring around each of the objects that would be attracted to a magnet.

steel drawing pin   iron radiator   rubber duck   copper pipe

aluminium window frame   stainless steel fork

wooden toy

1 Attractive puzzles

True or false?

	True	False
a Magnetism is an invisible force.		
b Magnets attract objects that are made from any material.		
c Two North poles will repel each other.		
d Unlike poles attract one another.		
e Unlike poles repel one another.		
f Magnets can't work through water.		
g It's possible to use a magnet to move a paper clip through a thin book.		

2 North or South?

Write 'S' or 'N' to show the poles on these magnets.

These magnets are attracted to each other.

These magnets are repelling one another.

On your toes

Are bigger magnets always stronger? _____

42

Light and shadow

Get started

Draw a picture here to show how your shadow is formed on the ground on a sunny day.

DON'T FORGET

Light can only travel in straight lines.

1 Light fantastic

Denise and Ed moved a torch further away from a toy. They were investigating how this would affect the **size** of the shadow cast by the toy. Here is a table showing the results of their investigation:

Distance between torch and toy (cm)	10	20	30	40
Size of shadow (cm)	80	65	53	48

a When is the shadow biggest? _____

b When is it smallest? _____

c Write a conclusion for this investigation.

_____

_____

2 Another investigation

Now Denise and Ed try investigating the length of shadows. They start with the torch down near the table and move it higher, always keeping it the same distance away from the toy. Complete their table by predicting roughly what you think the **length** of the shadow will be:

Height of the torch (cm)	5	20	35	50
Length of shadow (cm)	100			

Explain your predictions:

_____

_____

_____

Try doing this investigation yourself and see if your predictions were close.

On your toes

Why shadows often have fuzzy edges?

_____

_____

_____

43

Mirrors

Get started

Your reflection in a mirror **seems** to be as far behind the mirror as you are in front of it. On this drawing, draw where your reflection **seems** to be behind the mirror

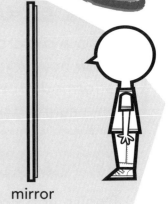

mirror

1 On reflection

Fill in the spaces using these words: predictable, same, bounces.

a When light shines on an object, it _____ off it in all directions.

b When light hits a reflective surface, like a mirror, it behaves in a

_____ way.

c If a beam of light hits a flat mirror at a particular angle, it bounces off the

mirror at the _____ angle, but in the opposite direction.

2 Look at this drawing of a periscope.

It is really an 's'-shaped tube with mirrors across the inside corners. Light enters the top. Show how the light will reflect off the mirrors to come out of the periscope at the bottom. Use a ruler and be accurate with your angles.

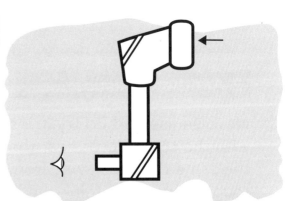

3 Draw lines between the names of the mirrors and their descriptions.

If you are not sure – look in a shiny spoon for help!

flat mirror	Curves out. Images look small.
concave mirror	Images look just like the object.
convex mirror	Curves in. Images look large.

On your toes

Shadows and reflections are the same thing. True or false? _____

Eyes and vision

Get started

True or false?

	True	False
a We see objects when light is reflected from them.		
b We can see objects which are around corners.		
c Objects which give out light are called light sources.		

1 An eye spy puzzle

Draw arrows to show how the child sees the sparkler.

2 Another eye spy puzzle

Draw arrows to show how the child sees the book.

3 Why should you never look directly at the Sun?

_____

_____

_____

On your toes

What can you see if it's totally dark? _____

Sounds and vibrations

Get started

Choose the correct answer

a Which of these would make a loud noise?
a large vibration/a small vibration

b Which of these would make a high noise?
a fast vibration/a slow vibration

DON'T FORGET

All sounds are made by something vibrating.

1 Sounds good!

Complete the flow chart to show what is happening in this picture.

The path of vibrations

Jane hits her drum
▼
a The _____ from the drum vibrate the _____ around it.
▼
b The vibrations _____ to Paul's drum through the _____ .
▼
c Paul's drum starts to _____ .
▼
d The _____ of Paul's drum shakes the rice on top.

2 Use lines to join the words to the correct explanation

pitch	The loudness of a sound.
volume	A solid, liquid or gas, through which sound can travel.
medium	A kind of shaking or wobbling.
vibration	This describes if sounds are high or low.

3 Draw a picture here showing how sound travels away from a bell.

On your toes

Why can't you hear sounds in space?

_____

Hearing

Get started

Why do some workers wear ear protectors?

_____

1 Hear hear!

DON'T FORGET

Sounds have to travel through something: a solid, liquid or gas.

This is a Native American tracker. What do you think he is doing?

_____

How can this happen?

_____

_____

2 What is wrong?

Tom and Heenal are disappointed. Their string telephones do not work. What is wrong?

_____

_____

_____

3 Whales can call to each other over vast distances.

How does this happen?

_____

_____

_____

On your toes

Why do you think that your outer ear is shaped in the way that it is?

_____

The Earth and the moon

Get started

The Earth's orbit around the sun isn't a perfect circle.

The shape of its orbit is an ellipse/eclipse.

1 A world of science

Fill in the missing words:

a The Earth travels around the _____ which takes _____ .

b The moon travels around the _____ which takes _____ .

c The Earth spins on its axis as it travels through space. It takes the Earth _____ to spin around once.

2 The phases of the moon

Here are drawings that show the phases of the moon at different times during one orbit of the Earth.

Write the correct label under each drawing: full moon, half moon or crescent moon.

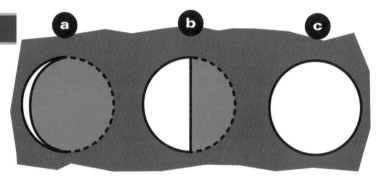

_____   _____   _____

3 A new moon

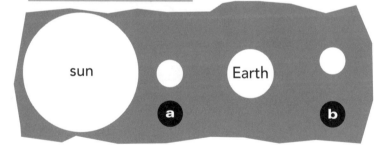

a Which position is the moon in when it is a 'new moon'? Tick **a** or **b** on the diagram to show your answer.

b Explain why this happens.

_____

_____

_____

On your toes

Why does it go dark at night time?

_____

48

Get started

Complete this sentence. As the Earth goes around the sun, it _____ on its axis.

1 Time to think

Put a circle around the statement that is false.

b The sun appears to move across the sky because the Earth is spinning in space.

a In the early morning, shadows are long.

d Shadows are at their shortest at midday.

c The Earth is still in space, and the sun moves around it.

2 Add the sun to this picture:

3 On this picture of the Earth, draw a person in each of these positions and label them with the correct letter:

a person in the night
b person at dawn
c person in daylight

On your toes

Why are shadows shortest at midday?

_____

49

Test paper

1 Tom's class were doing a project on 'Ourselves'. The children had to think about how they had changed since they were a baby.

What are the two parts of the human life cycle that Tom has been through already now he is a child? What is the next stage he will go through?

Write your answers in these spaces.

a _____

b _____

c _____

2 Josh doesn't like eating fruit or vegetables. Every day his mum puts some raw carrots, grapes, an apple or banana in his lunchbox with his sandwiches and crisps.

a Why is it important that Josh eats fruit and vegetables?

_____

b What does 'a balanced diet' mean?

_____

3 Inside our bodies we have a skeleton.

a What is our skeleton made from?

_____

b What does the skull protect?

_____

c What do the ribs protect?

_____

d What body parts join onto bones to help us move?

_____

e The skeleton protects organs and help us move. What other function does the skeleton have?

_____

4 Jamie has a packet of seeds. He makes a small hole in the soil in his garden and drops all the seeds into it.

At first lots of tiny green leaves appear, but they soon die. What went wrong?

_____

_____

_____

5 Describe how the bee helps to pollinate plants. Use these words to help you:

> **pollen   stamens   stigma**

_____

_____

_____

_____

6 How do you think these seeds of the dandelion and burdock plants are dispersed?

_____

_____

7 Complete this grid which can be used to classify animals.

	What is their skin like?	How do they breathe?	How do they reproduce?	Does their inside temperature stay steady?
amphibians	covered in scales	gills	lay eggs in water	no
reptiles	damp with no scales	young have gills but adults have lungs		no
birds	dry and scaly		lay eggs on land	no
		lungs	lay eggs on land	
	have fur or hair	lungs	give birth to live young	yes

8 Describe one way in which a leopard is adapted for its life in the rainforest.

_____

_____

9 Choose the right words to complete the sentence.
An endangered species is one which:

a ☐ kills other animals   **b** ☐ lives in high places   **c** ☐ is nearly extinct

10 Join each object to the right sorting circle.

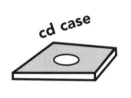
cd case

door

sandwich box
LUNCH

bag of flour
FLOUR

fir cone

clay

natural materials

man-made materials

11 Some children poured some hot soup into two different cups.
Every minute they measured the temperature of the soup.

a What do you think the children were trying to find out?

_____

_____

b One of the children noticed that there was more soup in one cup than the other. Did this matter?

_____

_____

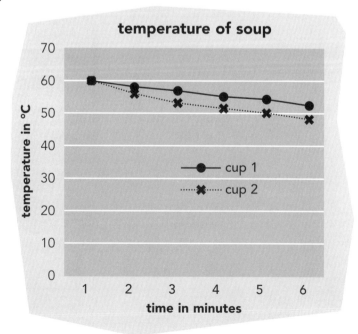

temperature of soup

temperature in °C

cup 1
cup 2

time in minutes

12 Alice likes to grow lilies because she likes their scent.
Here is a key which she uses to identify her lilies.

Does the flower have white petals?

yes

Are the flowers trumpet-shaped?

yes → Madonna lily

no → Golden-rayed lily

no

Do the petals have spots?

yes

Are the flowers open in August?

yes → Henry's lily

no → Orange lily

no → Coral lily

a What colour petals does a Madonna lily have? _____

b Alice would like a lily which bloomed in August.
Which one would be best? _____

c Alice liked lilies without spots best. Which one
should she choose? _____

sandy soil   clay soil

Water was poured onto these sieves of soil at the same time.
After a few minutes, the level of water in the bowls was recorded.
What difference would you expect to see?

_____

_____

14 Write a label by each arrow to say what is happening in this diagram of the water cycle.

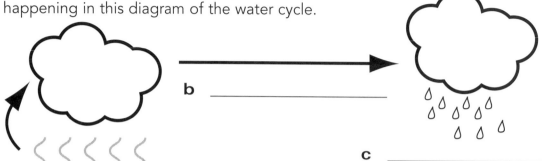

b _____

c _____

a _____

d _____

15 Use these words to fill in the gaps. Only use each word once.

solution	insoluble	soluble

a Sugar is _____ in water.

b A clear mixture of sugar and water is called a _____

c Sand is _____ in water.

16 Look at the following circuit drawings.

In which one would the bulb be bright? _____

In which one will the bulb be dim? _____

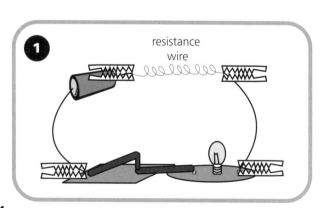

1 resistance wire

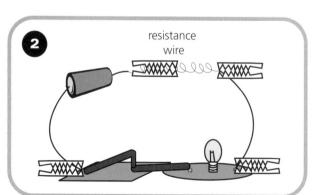

2 resistance wire

17 Look at these drawings where nothing is moving.

Draw arrows to show the forces acting in each one. Make sure you show the direction the forces are pushing or pulling.

18 a What's the name of the force which keeps you on Earth? _____

b Explain why you would weigh much less if you were on the moon.

_____

_____

19 You carry out an experiment where you weigh an object using a newton meter. You then lower the object into a bucket of water, and note that the weight is less in water. Why does this happen?

_____

_____

_____

_____

20 a What will happen to the shadow if Jack moves nearer to the screen?

_____

_____

b What will happen to the shadow if Jack moves nearer to the projector?

_____

_____

21 String telephones can transfer vibrations along a string so that sounds can be heard at the other end.

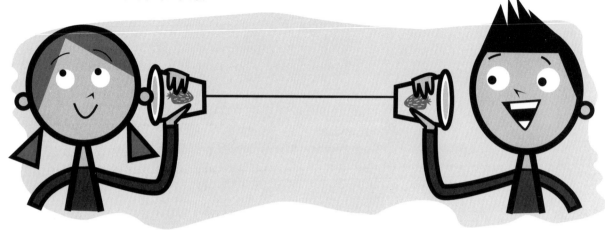

In an experiment to test which type of string transfers vibrations best, your friend changes the kind of string being used and the length of the string at the same time. What is wrong with what your friend has done?

_____

_____

_____

22 Some children put a stick in the ground and marked its shadow during the day.

a Why did the length of the shadow change during the day?

_____

_____

_____

b Why did the position of the shadow change during the day?

_____

_____

_____

Answers

Page 2

Get started
a growth
b reproduction
c movement
d nutrition
e sensitivity

1 a movement
  b reproduction
  c nutrition
  d growth
  e sensitivity

2 b Acorns fall off the trees
   in autumn.

On your toes
A plant takes nutrients in through its roots from the soil.

Page 3

Get started
reproduction

1 any three from:
  grown
  become more independent
  can walk
  can read
  can ride a bike, etc.

2 foetus, baby, child, teenager, adult

3 a true
  b true
  c true
  d false

On your toes
Humans would become extinct.

Page 4

Get started
a incisors
b molars
c canines

1
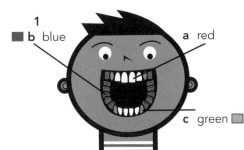
b blue   a red

c green

2 a Because he only cleans his teeth before breakfast and not after he has eaten.
  b Rita
  c Because she cleans her teeth after she has eaten and before she goes to bed.

On your toes
Any fruit or vegetable, especially apples or celery, dental gum, milk.

Page 5

Get started
A diet which has food from all food groups.

1 **Proteins** – to help us grow and repair parts of our body. Found in meat, fish, eggs, cheese, nuts, milk, beans
  Carbohydrates – to give us energy
  Fats and oils – found in butter, oils, cheese
  Vitamins and minerals – to keep us healthy. Found in fruit and vegetables
  Fibre – to move food through the gut and for healthy intestines

2 a vitamins and minerals, fibre
  b protein, fats and oils

On your toes
Your body will store the extra food as fat.

Page 6

Get started
function

organ	position	function
lungs	6	e
heart	5	c
brain	1	b
liver	2	d
kidney	3	a
digestive system	4	f

On your toes
kidneys
lungs

Page 7

Get started

Lungs
Heart
Body

1 b, d, a, g, c, e, f

On your toes
Oxygen and food. It also carries waste carbon dioxide back to the lungs.

Page 8

Get started
True:
muscles work harder
breathing gets faster
feel hot
feel sweaty
feel tired
heartbeat gets faster
body uses up oxygen to give energy
blood is pumped faster

1 a line A sitting reading; line B walking; line C skipping
  b The harder you are exercising, the faster the heart beats to carry oxygen around the body.

On your toes
To collect more oxygen from the air. Muscles need oxygen to get energy from food.

Page 9

Get started
brain → skull
spinal cord → backbone
heart → ribs

1
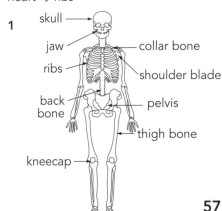
skull
jaw
ribs
back bone
kneecap
collar bone
shoulder blade
pelvis
thigh bone

2 blue endoskeletons –
human, elephant, cat,
hedgehog, rabbit, bird, fish
red exoskeletons – the rest

On your toes
3 To allow movement (because
muscles are attached to the
bones)

Page 10

Get started
a muscles
b pull
c blood, food
d faster, rate

1 a biceps
  b thicker
  c softer
  d oxygen

2
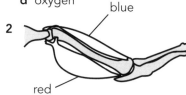
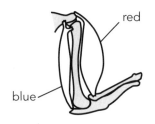

On your toes
Oxygen and food carried by blood.

Page 11

Get started
a false **b** true **c** false

1 b 'Smoking kills'
  c 'Don't play with drugs'
  a 'Don't drink and drive'

On your toes
tobacco

Page 12

Get started
a sun
b make food
c chlorophyll
d yellow

1 a plant 1
  b Because it will have light
    and water.
  c They will wither and drop off.
  d They will go yellow.
  e water, warmth, light,
    air, nutrients.

On your toes
Same size plant/same size
pot/same kind of plant.

Page 13

Get started
a leaves
b roots
c petals
d stem
e ovary

1 a The half of the stem in
    blue ink had turned blue,
    and the half in red ink
    had turned red.
  b The ink had travelled up
    the stem.

2 a B (marram grass)
  b Water is deeper down in
    sandy soil. Sandy soil blows
    about easily so the roots
    need to be deep and strong
    to hold the plant firmly in
    the soil.
  c To anchor the plant in the
    ground and to take up water.

On your toes
A tap root.

Page 14

Get started
To attract insects.

1 a false **b** true **c** false

2 a a petals, **b** sepal,
    c filament, **d** anther,
    e stigma, **f** style, **g** ovary

  b *male parts*   *female parts*
    anther   stigma
    filament   style
               ovary

On your toes
Ovules in the ovary.

Page 15

Get started
a anther
b male
c stigma
d seeds

1 d, c, b, a
  d A bee is attracted to a flower
    by the petals.
  c Pollen from the anthers sticks
    to the bee's legs and body.
  b The bee flies to a new flower.
  a The pollen from its legs and
    body sticks to the stigma of
    the second flower.

2 a Pollinating the tomatoes by
    carrying pollen from one
    flower to another.
  b wind or insects

On your toes
seeds

Page 16

Get started
a true **b** false **c** true

1 1 c, **2** d, **3** g, **4** f, **5** b, **6** e, **7** a

On your toes
seeds

Page 17

Get started
seeds: pea, bean, peanut
fruits: lemon, apple, tomato,
     cucumber

1 a 3, explosion – when the pod
    dries out it bursts open
  b 2, wind – the seeds are light
    and can be carried by the
    wind easily
  c 1, animals – birds eat the
    bright coloured fruit. There
    are lots of seeds within one
    fruit

d **1**, animals – the tiny little hooks get caught on the animals' fur

e **1**, animals – the brightness of a rosehip attracts birds and small mammals

f **2**, wind – the shape of the fruit helps it to be carried by the wind. It is also very light.

On your toes
Blown by the wind.

Page 18

Get started
water, warmth, air

1 **a** Ellie's
   b David's
   c No. The seedlings have long stems because they have been trying to reach the light.

On your toes
chlorophyll

Page 19

Get started
an invertebrate

1 **a** Reptiles lay their eggs on land.
   b Young amphibians breathe through gills.
   c Fish have a body covering of scales.
   d Mammals have babies that are born alive.
   e Birds are able to control the temperature of the inside of their bodies. They are warm blooded.

On your toes
Mammals produce milk to feed their babies.

Page 20

Get started
classifying

1 **a** running beaker
   b wooly leaper
   c big snapper
   d furry whistler
   e sleepy bird brain

On your toes
yes or no

Page 21

Get started
a environments
b habitat
c adaptation

1 **a** The polar bear would be easily seen. It would get too hot in its thick coat. The bear's food source would not be available.
   b The leopard would show up against the white snow. It would die of cold. The leopard's food source would not be available.

2 A hedgehog's body is covered in spines. They can roll in a ball to protect themselves.

3 The seal has a good shape for swimming. It has flippers. It has thick fat for keeping warm.

On your toes
a true   **b** false

Page 22

Get started
sparrow hawk
▲
shrew
▲
insect
▲
leaves

1 **a** producer
   b herbivore
   c predator

2 **a** wheat grains P, chicken C
   b hamster C, sunflower seeds P
   c termite C, piece of wood P
   d bamboo shoots P, giant panda C

3 Fieldmice. One owl would need to eat several mice.

On your toes
Because plants can store the Sun's energy in foods. Animals have to eat plants to get this stored energy.

Page 23

Get started
a pollution
b species
c extinct

1 **a** Animals can escape if gates are left open.
   b Litter can be dangerous to animals, and it spoils the environment for others.
   c If people pick the flowers of plants they cannot reproduce. Rare plants could die out.

2 **a** They are recycling materials by using a bottle bank.
   b Recycling means that materials are not wasted. They can be used again.

On your toes
They rot away and do not hurt animals if they are eaten (biodegradable).

Page 24

Get started
a false   **b** true   **c** false

1 **a** carbon dioxide
   b Nothing, the yeast will be unchanged in the bottom of the flask.
   c No bubbles because there is no sugar for the yeast to feed on.
   d In flask Y they would see bubbles of carbon dioxide. The gas will have blown the balloon up. Flask Z would only have a very few bubbles, if any, because yeast needs warmth to feed and grow.
   e Just yeast and sugar

On your toes
To stop micro-organisms from your hands getting on the food.

Page 25

Get started
made from

1 natural – shell, stone, wood,
   clay, wool, silk
   man made – plastic, nylon,
   polythene, polystyrene, lycra,
   polyester

2 **a** fired
   b minced and soaked
   c heated

On your toes
One which is man made.

Page 26

Get started
a making a tie
b making a magnetic door catch
c making a mop
d making a CD case

1

	transparent	rough	smooth
hard	glass	sandpaper	slate
soft	polythene	carpet wool	ribbon

2 **a** stretchy
   b transparent
   c heavy

On your toes
properties

Page 27

Get started
hot to cold

1 **a** false, **b** true, **c** true, **d** false,
   e true, **f** true, **g** true

2 **a** Rob
   b Newspaper is an insulator.
   It will keep heat away from
   the lolly.

On your toes
plastic

Page 28

Get started
ground

1 **a** smooth and breaks into flat
   pieces
   b soft and white

   c hard and beautifully coloured
   d hard-wearing and strong

2 **a** permeable **b** impermeable

3 **a** rock B **b** rock C

On your toes
fossils

Page 29

Get started
a rock
b plants and animals
c air
d water

1 Burglar Ben

2 **a** pebbles or gravel
   b plant remains

On your toes
The remains of plants and animals.

Page 30

Get started
a true **b** false **c** true

1 solids – ice, cold butter, flour,
   play-dough
   liquids – engine oil, paint,
   vinegar, milk
   gases – oxygen, steam,
   exhaust fumes, air

2 **a** liquid, **b** solid, **c** gas

On your toes
Sand is millions of tiny pieces
of solid.

Page 31

Get started
a gas **b** solid

1 **a** boiling
   b melting
   c condensing
   d freezing
   e evaporation

2 **a** boiling – turning to from
   liquid to gas (steam)
   b melting – turning from solid
   to liquid

   c condensing – turning from
   gas to liquid.
   d freezing – turning from liquid
   to solid.

3 **a** evaporates
   b condenses
   c sea

On your toes
steam

Page 32

Get started
a permanent **b** permanent

1 **a** permanent
   b reversible
   c reversible
   d permanent

2 5:
   the alpha fuel froze in the
   fuel pods
   the water was boiling
   condensed into streams
   of water
   metal shields were melting
   somehow solidified again

On your toes
false

Page 33

Get started
true

1 **a** dissolving
   b solution
   c soluble
   d insoluble

2 **a**

   b

green
colour

On your toes
true

Page 34

Get started
a sieving
b filtering
c evaporating

1 a true
  b false
  c false
  d true

2 a Rock salt is added to water and stirred. The salt dissolves.
  b The mixture is poured into a funnel with filter paper in it. Small stones and sand get caught in the filter paper and salt solution goes through the paper into the beaker.
  c The salt solution is poured from the beaker into a dish.
  d Water vapour evaporates from the salt solution.
  e Salt crystals are left in the dish.

On your toes
saturated

Page 35

Get started

1 a

You could also have added a different circuit component such as an extra bulb or motor.

b

c cells
  Any two from: a bulb, a motor or a buzzer.

d

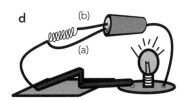

On your toes
A switch made from a paper clip that you can connect across the gap in the circuit.

Page 36

Get started
There is a gap in the circuit.

1 battery
  bulb
  buzzer
  motor
  switch off
  switch on

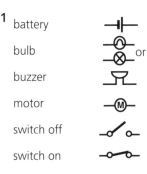
or

2 The cell has been short circuited. (The electricity can get back to the cell without going through any component. The cell will be damaged. It would eventually overheat and could cause a fire.)

3 This circuit has three cells connected to a bulb and a buzzer. There is a switch in the circuit that is on.

On your toes
A series circuit has all the components in a line.

Page 37

Get started
start to move, stop moving, change direction, speed up or slow down

1 a

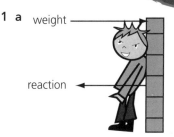
weight
reaction

b

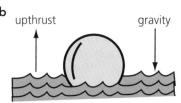
upthrust
gravity

c The weight of the toy is partly supported by the upthrust of the water.

On your toes
false (upthrust always pushes up)

Page 38

Get started
friction

1 The best way to show forces in operation is to draw arrows. The size and direction of the arrow shows the size and direction of the force.

2 a

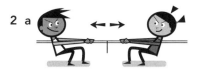

b

c

d

On your toes
true

Page 39

Get started
a attraction
b orbit, orbit
c pull, centre

1 Earth – because it's the largest of the three planets so it has the greatest gravitational pull.

2 The ball and the apple are being pulled downwards. The person skipping always comes back down when they leap into the air. The person on the skateboard is going down the slope because of the pull of gravity.

On your toes
False. Gravity gives you your weight.

Page 40

Get started
a false b true c false

1 a Different surfaces give different amounts of frictional force.
b sandpaper

2 a 25 × 25cm
b There is more air under larger parachutes as they fall. This means that the air resistance, the force that is trying to stop the parachute falling, is larger too. So, the bigger parachutes take longer to fall.

On your toes
They have streamlined shapes that cut through air resistance.

Page 41

Get started
The forces are equal.
The toy is not moving.

1 Isaac Newton

2 a 1N, b 3N, c 2N, d 5N

3

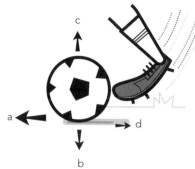

On your toes
circuit

Page 42

Get started
steel drawing pin, iron radiator, stainless steel fork

1 a true, b false, c true, d true, e false, f false, g true

2

On your toes
no

Page 43

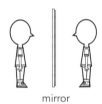

Get started
1 a When the torch is closest to the object.
b When the torch is furthest away from the object.
c A torch shining on an object creates a shadow. The nearer the torch is to the object, the bigger the shadow. When an object is closer to a light source more light is blocked out.

2 Your predictions should show the length of the shadow getting shorter each time. The reason is that, as the light source gets higher, the angle at which the light shines on the object changes. This will change the length (and shape) of the shadow.

On your toes
Because light is nearly always coming from a spread-out source, or from several sources at once.

Page 44

Get started
Your drawing should show that your reflection seems to be as far behind the mirror as you are in front of it.

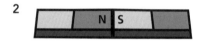

mirror

1 a bounces
b predictable
c same

2

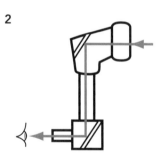

3

flat mirror — Images look just like the object.
concave mirror — Curves in. Images look large.
convex mirror — Curves out. Images look small.

On your toes
false

Page 45

Get started
a true, **b** false, **c** true

1

2

3 The strong light from the sun can damage the delicate parts of your eyes.

On your toes
nothing

Page 46

Get started
a a large vibration
b a fast vibration

1 a vibrations, air
 b travel, air
 c vibrate
 d vibration

2

pitch — This describes if sounds are high or low.
volume — The loudness of a sound.
medium — A solid, liquid or gas, through which sound can travel.
vibration — A kind of shaking or wobbling.

3 Your picture should show that sound travels from the bell in all directions.

On your toes
Because there is no atmosphere, and so no medium through which sound waves their travel.

Page 47

Get started
Because loud sounds can damage the delicate parts of our ears.

1 The tracker is listening to the sounds of the horse's hooves travelling through the solid ground. Sound vibrations can travel through solids.

2 The string between the phones needs to be taut for the sound vibrations to travel through it.

3 Sound vibrations travel well through water.

On your toes
To collect sounds and direct them down to the inside of your ear.

Page 48

Get started
ellipse

1 a sun – a year
 b Earth – a month (28 days)
 c a day (24 hours)

2 a crescent moon
 b half moon
 c full moon

3 a a
 b Because sunlight is falling on the side of the moon facing away from us. We can only see the dark side of the moon.

On your toes
Because our part of the Earth is facing away from the sun.

Page 49

Get started
spins

1 c

2

3

On your toes
Because the sun is at its highest point in the sky and shines directly down on things.

Test paper

1 a foetus, **b** baby, **c** teenager

2 a Because fruits and vegetables give us vitamins and minerals
 b A diet which has all the kinds of food we need – and not too much of any!

3 a bone
 b brain
 c heart and lungs
 d muscles
 e Support – the skeleton allows us to stand upright and holds all body parts in place.

4 The seeds were too crowded. Each seedling needs its own space to get light, air and water.

5 The bee visits flowers to collect pollen to make honey.
When the bee is in the flower, pollen from the stamens brushes onto the bee's body and legs.
When the bee goes to a new flower, the pollen brushes off onto the stigma of the new flower.

6 The dandelion seed is in a very light case, shaped like a feathery parachute which is blown about in the wind.
The case of the burdock seed is covered in little hooks which catch in the fur of animals.

7 The missing items on the grid are:
Fish
Amphibians – lay eggs in water
Reptiles – lungs
Birds – have feathers; yes
Mammals

8 Any of the following:
- spotted coat gives camouflage
- strong teeth for eating meat
- strong claws for gripping prey
- tail for balancing as it leaps or moves through trees
- strong legs for running and pouncing
- good eyesight

9 c is nearly extinct

10 natural materials:
door, bag of flour, fir cone, clay
man-made materials:
cd case, sandwich box

11 a Which materials kept the soup hottest for longer.
or Which material is the best insulator.
or Which materials made the best soup container.
b Yes. If the cups did not have the same amount of soup in them it was not a fair test.

12 a white
b Henry's lily
c Coral lily

13 Water would drain quickly through the sandy soil into the bowl.
Water would not drain through the clay soil and would make a puddle on the top of it.
So I would expect to see water in the bowl under the sandy soil, and none or very little in the bowl under the clay soil.

14 a Water evaporates from the sea to make clouds.
b The clouds are blown over the land.
c Water from the clouds condenses to make rain.
d The rain collects in rivers and is taken back to the sea.

15 a soluble
b solution
c insoluble

16 The bulb will be bright in circuit 2 because the electricity does not have to travel through all of the resistance wire.
The bulb will be dim in circuit 1 because the electricity has to work hard to travel through all of the resistance wire.

17

gravity

upforce

pull from team this side of rope pull from team this side of rope

18 a gravity
b You would weigh less on the moon because it is smaller than the Earth, so its gravitational pull is smaller.

19 The brick is partly supported by the upthrust of the water, so it pulls down less on the Newton meter.

20 a The shadow will get smaller.
b The shadow will grow larger

21 You should only change one variable in an investigation, everything else should stay the same. They should have changed either the kind of string or the length.

22 a The shadow would be long when the sun was low in the sky. It would be short when the sun was high in the sky. This is because of the angle at which the sunlight hit the stick.
b The shadow would move around the stick as the Earth moves around the sun. The sunlight will hit the stick from different directions.